PRAYERS
for Children

PRAYERS FOR CHILDREN
Copyright © 2005 by Good Books, Intercourse, PA 17534
International Standard Book Number: 1-56148-470-9
Library of Congress Catalog Card Number: 2004021152

Text compilation copyright © 2005 Rebecca Winter
Illustrations copyright © 2005 Helen Cann
Original edition published in English under the title
The Lion Book of Prayers for Children.
Copyright © Lion Publishing 2005.

North American edition entitled
Prayers for Children
published by Good Books, 2005. All rights reserved.

Printed and bound in India

Library of Congress Cataloging-in-Publication Data

Prayers for children / written and compiled by Rebecca Winter ; illustrations by Helen
Cann.
   p. cm.
Includes indexes.
ISBN 1-56148-470-9 (hardcover)
1. Christian children–Prayer-books and devotions–English. I. Winter, Rebecca. II.
Cann, Helen, 1969-
BV265.P762 2005
242'.82–dc22   2004021152

PRAYERS
for Children

Written and compiled by Rebecca Winter

Illustrations by Helen Cann

Good Books

Intercourse, PA 17534
800/762-7171
www.goodbks.com

For Phillip, Lydia and Harry,
and with thanks to Chrystel Pattendon   R.W.

For Sara Pennant-Jones,
my almost-twin, with much love   H.C.

Contents

Introduction

 Have you ever wondered what God is like? What pictures come to mind when you think of God? For many of us the idea of God as a remote, strict policeman or ruler makes prayer difficult. We can't help feeling the need to make deals with God—for example, we promise to be good if we can just do well in our exams. And sometimes we may feel that we are simply not good enough for God to hear our prayers.

But God is not a remote instructor shouting directions from the distance. God gave the world an insight into what he is like by sending Jesus. Through Jesus we know that God's love is stronger than anything else and that God is with us, each of us, whoever we are.

Prayer is how we link ourselves to God, and as we tune our hearts and minds to God's way, we begin to feel God's arm around our shoulders and sense the way God wants us to go. We have to walk closely with him as our Guide; we will not know the way if we stand apart. But God draws us closer, moving us to pray. Our response to God is prayer.

There are many different ways of praying. The most obvious, and the place where most of us start, is by speaking. Talking out loud to God, either in our own words or by using prayers written by other people, helps us to feel that we are communicating; it's what we do person to person. Through written prayers we realize, too, that others have made this journey before us, and we can be inspired, challenged, informed. Certain prayers can become our favorites when we are unable to form our own thoughts or words.

There are many other ways of praying. So although this book contains a great many words, it contains spaces, too. These places for reflection are designed to stimulate our own quietness and openness to God. Focused stillness of this kind can be the most effective way of coming closer to God. The pictures throughout the book, particularly those at the beginning of each section, are there to make us pause, to ponder and to encourage our prayers.

Rebecca Winter

Here
I Am, God

God in Quietness

In a world full of noise, a place of silence can be hard to find. But we can find quietness, if we seek it, and here we can discover the inner stillness that will help us to be aware of God.

Where is your quiet place?
It might be in your room
or at a grandparent's house
or in your garden or on a favorite park bench.
Maybe you can find inner quiet as you ride your bike
or go high on a swing?

Where is God?

God is where you are.

Be still, then, and know that God is here.

Dear God,

Help me to find a quiet place where I can be still

and think of you.

Amen

Come to us, Lord God, as we come to you in prayer.

Be with us now, we pray, and guide the words we share.

It is not far to go

for you are near.

It is not far to go

for you are here.

And not by traveling, Lord,

we come to you,

but by the way of love,

and we love you.

Amy Carmichael (1868–1951)

When I feel alone Your Presence is ever with me.

Come, Holy Dove, cover with love.

When I feel weak your strength will seek me.

Come, Holy Dove, cover with love.

Spirit be about my head,

Spirit peace about me shed,

Spirit light about my way,

Spirit guardian night and day.

Come, Holy Dove,

Cover with love.

David Adam

Lord, make my heart a place where angels sing!

John Keble (1792–1866)

Good shepherd, lead me to the place where
I can be closest to you.

When I see the birds go soaring,

wheeling, dipping through the sky,

deep inside my spirit longs to learn to fly.

Lois Rock

Dear God,

Help me to find an open space where I can shout
and sing and dance my prayers to you.

To you, O Lord, I lift up my soul.

Psalm 25:1

I hold up my arms and smile at the sky,
stretching up, feeling your spirit in the wind.
Thank you, God.

Sue Atkinson

Sometimes, God, the world feels too busy.

Sometimes it feels as if everyone wants too much from me.

Sometimes I feel really stressed.

Sometimes I want to scream...

Show me how to trust in you,

Show me your way of peace.

O God of peace,
lift us, we pray, to your presence,
where we may be still
and know that you are God.

Send out your light, Lord,
send your truth to be our guide,
then let them lead us
to the place where you reside.

The Iona Community

Calm me, O Lord, as you stilled the storm,
Still me, O Lord, keep me from harm.
Let all the storms within me cease,
Enfold me, Lord, in your peace.

A Celtic prayer

Thank you, God,
for being where we are.

Lord, teach us to pray.

From the Gospel of Luke

Listening God,

thank you that when

speaking with you

we are not approaching

a harsh boss

but a loving friend.

Amen

Listen Lord, listen Lord, not to our words

but to our prayer. You alone, you alone,

understand and care.

The Iona Community

Dear God,

Guide our thinking and our praying.

Amen

Here I am, God, this is me,

lift my spirit, set me free.

Take my dreams, my hopes and plans,

hold my future in your hands.

God be in my head, and in my understanding;

God be in my eyes, and in my looking;

God be in my mouth, and in my speaking;

God be in my heart, and in my thinking;

God be at my end, and at my departing.

From a Book of Hours (1514)

Let me hear of your steadfast love in the morning,
for in you I put my trust.
Teach me the way I should go,
for to you I lift up my soul.

Psalm 143:8

Lord Jesus, you prayed to your Father, "Do what you
want, not what I want." Help us to follow your example.
Help us to want to do the things that please you and to
go the way that you have chosen for us.
Amen

Mary Batchelor

Lord, take our minds and think through them;
take our lips and speak through them;
take our hearts and set them on fire
with the desire to do your holy will.
Amen

A student prayer

God, this is your world,

You made us,

You love us;

Teach us how to live

In the world that you have made.

Hope Freeman

Dear God,

There are many paths to choose from.

Please show me the way to go.

Amen

Not my works
But your work

Not my perfection
But yours

Not my grasp
But your grip

Not my completeness
But yours

Not my strength
But your strength

Not my honesty
But yours

Not my trust
But your truth

Not my will be done
But yours.

Steve Turner

Think through me thoughts of God;
My Father, quiet me,
Till in thy holy presence, hushed,
I think thy thoughts of thee.

Think through me thoughts of God,
That always, everywhere,
The stream that through my being flows
May homeward pass in prayer.

Think through me thoughts of God,
And let my own thoughts be
Lost like the sand-pools on the shore
Of the eternal sea.

Amy Carmichael (1868–1951)

O God, surely my help and my prayers are simply a drop in the ocean of need. But then I think how an ocean is made up of tiny drops.

H ow shall I not give you all that I have, when you, in your great goodness, give me all that you are?

Author unknown

Bless to me, O God,
the work of my hands.
Bless to me, O God,
the work of my mind.
Bless to me, O God,
the work of my heart.

Author unknown

I am only me, but I'm still someone.
I cannot do everything, but I can do something.
Just because I cannot do everything
does not give me the right to do nothing.

Motto from an Amish school in Pennsylvania

Lord God, help me to walk in the light
and to be a light to others.
Amen

Who is there on land?
Who is there on wave?
Who is there on billow?
Who is there by door-post?
Who is along with us?
God and Lord.

From *Carmina Gadelica*

God before me, God behind me,
God above me, God below me;
I on the path of God,
God upon my track.

From *Carmina Gadelica*

I go forth today
in the might of heaven,
in the brightness of the sun,
in the whiteness of snow,
in the splendor of fire,
in the speed of lightning,
in the swiftness of wind,
in the firmness of rock.
I go forth today
in the hand of God.

An Irish prayer (8th century)

I lift up my eyes to the hills—
from where will my help come?
My help comes from the Lord,
who made heaven and earth.

Psalm 121:1–2

Without you, God, I am like a rudderless ship.

God says:

I will look after you because I made you.

I won't let you fall over—I will show you the way to go.

I'll look after you while you sleep, I'll sit beside your bed.

I won't smother you, but I will keep an eye on you.

I'll provide all you need—the sun and moon are mine to command!

I will let you live your life, I won't interfere, but I'll keep in touch,
   show an interest, make suggestions, offer guidance when necessary,
      be concerned.

Wherever you go I will be there for you because you are my
   precious child.

I want you to stand on your own two feet, to use the intelligence
   I gave you to make decisions, act wisely, to be mature, bold and
      courageous.

But don't forget you are still my child and you can come to me to
   be held, loved, to cry on my shoulder.

I will never undermine you, manipulate you or put you down.

You will never disappoint me by being yourself.

My only ambition is that you may live as a child of light, of joy,
   in this world and the next.

Rowena Edlin-White, inspired by Psalm 121

Morning
Has Broken

Morning has broken
Like the first morning,
Blackbird has spoken
Like the first bird.
Praise for the singing!
Praise for the morning!
Praise for them, springing
From the first Word.

Eleanor Farjeon (1881–1965)

Dear Lord my God,
Good morning!
The rain is falling
to wake the wintry world,
to green the grass,
to bring blossoms to the tree
   outside my window.
The world and I wake up for you.
Alleluia!

Madeleine L'Engle

Waking, each dawn, I greet the morning.

Expectantly open my eyes.

Each day I'm living, a gift that I'm given.

Can't wait to see the sun rise.

Dave Andrews

Remind me each morning

of your constant love,

for I put my trust in you.

Psalm 143:8

This morning, God,
This is your day.
I am your child,
Show me your way.

Author unknown

Dear Lord Jesus, we shall have this day only once;
before it is gone, help us to do all the good we can,
so that today is not a wasted day.

Stephen Grellet (1773–1855)

Creator God, we thank you for this day. We thank
you for all the opportunities it gives us to be the
people you want us to be. Help us to stay within the
sunshine of your love.

Let this day, O Lord, add some knowledge or good
deed to yesterday.

Lancelot Andrewes (1555–1626)

Loving God,
I am scared of today.
I want to hide here
and not move.

Loving God,
I ask you to be with me today.
I want to put my hand in yours
and move on.
Amen

Dear God,
This is the day I have dreaded.
Please give me all that I need to get
through today.
Amen

I have been crying in the night, O God;

my pillow is wet with tears.

I am too tired to face the day,

too scared to face those who hate me.

Keep me safe from those evil people;

listen to my cry for help.

Bring all their wickedness to an end;

answer my prayer.

Lois Rock, based on Psalm 6

I really messed up everything yesterday.

Please help me to say sorry.

Please help me to forgive others and forgive myself.

Help me now to start again, everything new, with

your love flowing over me as I try to live for you.

Sue Atkinson

For the clean sheet of paper that is today, I thank you, God.

For the smudges and crossings out of yesterday, I am sorry.

Guide my hand as the story of this new day is written.

Fill me with joy and gladness.

Awake, O my soul, awake.

Joy comes in the morning.

I will be your eternal light.

Praise God with shouts of joy.

Arise, shine out, for your light has come.

My saving power will rise on you like the sun.

The Lord, my God, lights up my darkness.

A Psalm for Africa

O praise God in his holy place,
Praise him in the sky our tent,
Praise him in the earth our mother;
Praise him for his mighty works,
Praise him for his marvelous power.

Praise him with the beating of great drums,
Praise him with the horn and rattle;
Praise him in the rhythm of the dance,
Praise him in the clapping of the hands;
Praise him in the stamping of the feet,
Praise him in the singing of the chant.

Praise him with the rushing of great rivers,
Praise him with the music of the wind;
Praise him with the swaying of tall trees,
Praise him with the singing of the sea.
Praise him, the one on whom we lean and do not fall;
Let everything that has breath praise the Lord.

Author unknown

You are holy, Lord, the only God,

and your deeds are wonderful.

You are strong, you are great,

you are the most high, you are almighty.

You, holy Father, are King of heaven and earth.

You are Three and One, Lord God, all good.

You are good, all good, supreme good,

Lord God, living and true.

You are love, you are wisdom.

You are humility, you are endurance.

You are rest, you are peace.

You are joy and gladness, you are justice and moderation.

You are all our riches, and you suffice for us.

You are beauty, you are gentleness.

You are our protector, you are our guardian and defender.

You are our courage, you are our haven and our hope.

You are our faith, our great consolation.

You are our eternal life, great and wonderful Lord,

God almighty, merciful Savior.

St. Francis of Assisi (1182–1226)

If my lips could sing as many songs

as there are waves in the sea:

if my tongue could sing as many hymns

as there are ocean billows:

if my mouth filled the whole firmament with praise:

if my face shone like the sun and moon together:

if my hands were to hover in the sky like powerful eagles

and my feet ran across mountains as swiftly as the deer;

all that would not be enough

to pay you fitting tribute,

O Lord my God.

A Jewish prayer

Dear God,

You are greater than anything

I can see or imagine.

Su Box

All you swooping gulls on high,
praise the Lord.
All you waves crashing at the shore,
praise the Lord.
All you fish in the ocean's depths,
praise the Lord.
And you sun above
and you sand below,
praise the Lord.

Lord God, we want to thank you
for all the goodness and beauty
in the world. We praise your holy name.

In the singing of birds
Is the sound of God.
In the swimming of fish
Is the power of God.
In the moving of beasts
Is the willing of God.
In the heart of humankind
Is the dwelling of God.

In my heart and my head,
In my hands and my feet,
God's Spirit within me
Shall move and shall speak.

Evelyn Francis Capel

Creator God, I'm astonished by the beauty in the world.
Butterflies with blue and purple in their wings,
the daring reds and oranges on the flowers,
baby birds who flutter their wings, waiting to be fed,
and a million stars.
You truly are a Great Creator!

Sue Atkinson

Give to me, Lord God, eyes that I may see
the wonders of your creation.

Give to me, Lord God, ears that I may hear
the music of your world.

Give to me, Lord God, lips that I may share
my thankfulness and praise.

Give to me, Lord God, a heart of love
to treasure all these things.

Your beauty can be seen all around me, Creator God,
help me to be part of all that is good in the world.

There is no bird on the wing,
There is no star in the sky,
There is nothing beneath the sun,
But proclaims his goodness.

From *Carmina Gadelica*

Praise for Our World

Most high, most great and good Lord, to you belong praises, glory and every blessing; to you alone do they belong, most high God.

May you be blessed, my Lord, for the gift of all your creatures and especially for our brother sun, by whom the day is enlightened. He is radiant and bright, of great splendor, bearing witness to you, O my God.

May you be blessed, my Lord, for our sister the moon and the stars; you have created them in the heavens, fair and clear.

May you be blessed, my Lord, for our brother the wind, for the air, for cloud and calm, for every kind of weather, for through them you sustain all creatures.

May you be blessed, my Lord, for our sister water, which is very useful, humble, pure and precious.

May you be blessed, my Lord, for our brother fire, bright, noble and beautiful, untamable and strong, by whom you illumine the night.

May you be blessed, my Lord, for our mother the earth, who sustains and nourishes us, who brings forth all kinds of fruit, herbs and brightly colored flowers.

St. Francis of Assisi (1182–1226), "Canticle of the Sun"

Thank you, God, for the morning light,
the sunshine bright over this city.
Thank you for all the energy and life in
these buildings, in these streets.
The early morning rush has begun,
the world is awake.
Go with me, God, as I go down
to join the day.

Loving God, help me to see you in the
people I meet today. Help me to hear you
above the noise of the traffic. Help me to
feel your presence in this busy day.

O Lord, may I be directed what
to do and what to leave undone.

Elizabeth Fry (1780–1845)

Teach me, my God and King,
In all things thee to see;
And what I do in anything,
To do it as for thee.

George Herbert (1593–1633)

Who knows what will happen today?
You know and you care.
Thank you, God.

This is the day the Lord has made;
let us rejoice and be glad in it.

Psalm 118:24

We thank you, God, for all the goodness and beauty we encounter.
We thank you for new green shoots, the buds, the blossom, the
tadpoles in the pond, the clear, crisp sunshine calling the earth
back to life. We thank you for this life, this love.

For the treasure of the garden, the gilly-flowers of gold,
The prouder petalled tulips, the primrose full of spring,
For the crowded orchard boughs, and the swelling buds that hold
A yet unwoven wonder, to thee our praise we bring.

John Drinkwater (1882–1936)

Creator God, today I watched an ant
carrying a seed four times its size.
You made an amazing world!

Sue Atkinson

Dear God,
Help us to find the time to stop and stare, to pause and wonder.
Amen

Maybe it was the sun on my back,
or the gentle slope of the track,
or the nest that we found,
or the foxgloves tall on the forest ground.
I don't know how, but my heart feels free,
Thank you, God, for walking with me.

All things bright and beautiful,
All creatures great and small,
All things wise and wonderful,
The Lord God made them all.

He gave us eyes to see them,
And lips that we may tell
How great is God Almighty,
Who has made all things well.

Mrs. C.F. Alexander (1818–95)

If you get simple beauty and naught else,
you get about the best thing God invents.

Robert Browning (1812–89)

He prayeth best, who loveth best
All things both great and small;
For the dear God who loveth us,
He made and loveth all.

S.T. Coleridge (1772–1834)

For the beauty of the earth,
For the beauty of the skies,
For the love which from our birth
Over and around us lies:
Lord of all, to thee we raise
This, our sacrifice of praise.

For the beauty of each hour,
Of the day and of the night,
Hill and vale and tree and flower,
Sun and moon and stars of light:
Lord of all, to thee we raise
This, our sacrifice of praise.

F.S. Pierpoint (1835–1917)

Beauty is God's handwriting. Welcome it in every fair face,
every fair day, every fair flower.

Charles Kingsley (1819–75)

Praise God for the animals—
for the colors of them,
for the spots and stripes of them,
for the patches and plains of them,
their claws and paws.

Lynne Warren

Thank you for the beasts so tall.
Thank you for the creatures small.
Thank you for all things that live.
Thank you, God, for all you give.

H.W. Dobson

Dear God, please bless all creatures,
the big ones and the small;
the loud ones and the fierce ones,
and those not heard at all.

We pray for animals who are suffering because of human
cruelty and greed. May such injustice be brought to light.
Please be with those who work on behalf of animals.

A rainbow makes me feel as if heaven has
come down to earth. Thank you, God.

How did you make the rainbow
And what is beyond the sky?
Why did you make the sun so hot,
And what makes the clouds race by?
You are the Lord, the Creator.
Only you know how and why.

Elizabeth Laird

In every rainbow there is the same loving promise
that God gave to Noah.

Kenneth Steven

O joy that seekest me through pain,
I cannot close my heart to thee;
I trace the rainbow through the rain,
and feel the promise is not vain,
that morn shall tearless be.

George Matheson (1842–1906)

Praying Without Words

Sometimes you want to pray but can't find the right words. Maybe you are feeling very sad or bubbling over with joy. Did you know that you can pray without words or do something to show God how you feel?

Sit by a window and watch the world, thinking of the people out there who help others, thinking of the beautiful world that God created. Even on a rainy day when you have to stay indoors, you can think of all the people who are glad of the rain and you can keep a lookout for rainbows.

Why not paint a picture, thinking of your feelings and the things that worry you? You don't need to decide to paint anything in particular. Just paint using whatever colors you want and let your paintbrush wander over the paper in whatever shape it wants to. How your picture turns out and what colors you choose may tell you something about how you are feeling. You can pray about your feelings, thanking God for your happiness, or asking for God's help with any anger or sadness.

Go for a walk to find something beautiful, maybe a butterfly or a flower, or maybe you will be able to see swallows up in the sky catching insects. All of these creatures point to the Great Creator who made the earth and loves and cares for everything.

Sue Atkinson

God of all creation, your love goes on forever, never stopping, always holding,

Sue Atkinson

Starry Night

Lord, you created the day and the night,

you created darkness and light.

We commend to you this day

all that has happened in it.

Protect us through the night

until the morning light.

David Adam

God is at the anvil, beating out the sun;

Where the molten metal spills,

At his forge among the hills

He has hammered out the glory of a day's that's done.

God is at the anvil, welding golden bars;

In the scarlet-streaming flame

He is fashioning a frame

For the shimmering silver beauty of the evening stars.

Lew Sarett

Blessed are you, O Lord our God,

King of the universe!

At your word night falls.

In your wisdom you open heaven's gates,

you control the elements and rotate the seasons.

You set the stars in the vault of heaven.

You created night and day.

You cause the light to fade when darkness comes

and the darkness to melt away in the light of the new day.

O ever-living and eternal God,

you will always watch over us, your creatures.

Blessed are you, O Lord,

at whose word night falls.

A Jewish prayer

This night is yours, and we are yours;

You are our Father, Brother, Friend.

Your love enfolds your children now,

This night, tomorrow, without end.

Lilian Cox

Bless the Lord, sun and moon:
Bless the Lord, you stars of heaven:
Sing his praise forever.

Dear God,
A blanket of black covers the sky
and I wonder how and I wonder why
so many questions fill my head
as I lie awake in my lonely bed.
You who set the moon and stars above
cover me now with your heavenly love.

The lightning and thunder
They go and they come;
But the stars and the stillness
Are always at home.

George MacDonald (1824–1905)

Dear God,

When I look up at the night sky and see the patterns of the stars
in the never-ending darkness, I feel amazed at the magnificent
beauty of your creation. I look out at the sea of blackness and
thank you for your love.

How wonderful, O Lord, are the works of your hands!
The heavens declare your glory,
the arch of the sky displays your handiwork.
In your love you have given us the power
to behold the beauty of your world
in all its splendor.

An excerpt from a Jewish prayer

God of all time,
Let us remember that life goes on when
darkness falls...

The owl calls majestically from high in the trees.

The bat darts to and fro in the deep blue sky.

The fox gathers food for her hungry young.

The nurse talks quietly to a restless child.

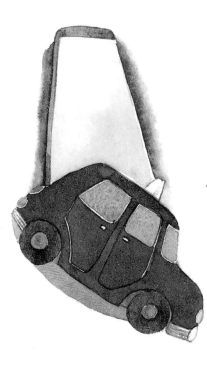

The taxi driver cruises through the empty streets.

The security guard makes a final check.

God of all time,
For these, and all those awake at night,
we ask for your protection.
Amen

The day is past, the sun is set,
And the white stars are in the sky;
While the long grass with dew is wet,
And through the air the bats now fly.

The lambs have now lain down to sleep,
The birds have long since sought their nests;
The air is still; and dark, and deep
On the hillside the old wood rests.

Yet of the dark I have no fear,
But feel as safe as when 'tis light;
For I know God is with me there,
And He will guard me through the night.

For He who rules the stars and sea,
Who makes the grass and trees to grow,
Will look on a poor child like me,
When on my knees I to Him bow.

He holds all things in His right hand,
The rich, the poor, the great, the small;
When we sleep, or sit, or stand,
Is with us, for He loves us all.

Thomas Miller (1807–74)

The sun will no more be your light by day,
nor will the brightness of the moon shine on you,
for the Lord will be your everlasting light,
and your God will be your glory.
Your sun will never set again,
and your moon will wane no more;
the Lord will be your everlasting light,
and your days of sorrow will end.

Isaiah 60:19–20

Dear God,
In the darkness of my loss I come
to you. I can't believe what has
happened. I don't know what to
do or say. Be with me in my sorrow
and protect me from my fear.
Amen

O God, where tears fall and hearts
are broken, enter the darkness with
the light of your love.

There are stars up above,
    so far away we only see their light long,
    long after the star itself is gone.
And so it is with people that we loved.
Their memories keep shining
    ever brightly
    though their time with us is done....
As we live our days these days we remember,
    we remember.

A Jewish prayer

Dear God,
Thank you for turning our sunsets
into sunrises.
Amen

God's Loving Care

The Lord is my shepherd;
I have everything I need.
He lets me rest in fields of green grass
 and leads me to quiet pools of fresh water.
He gives me new strength.
He guides me in the right paths,
 as he has promised.
Even if I go through the deepest darkness,
I will not be afraid, Lord,
for you are with me.
Your shepherd's rod and staff protect me.
You prepare a banquet for me,
where all my enemies can see me;
you welcome me as an honored guest
and fill my cup to the brim.
I know that your goodness and love will be
 with me all my life;
and your house will be my home as long
 as I live.

Psalm 23

Dear God, you are my shepherd.
You give me all I need.
You take me where the grass grows green
And I can safely feed.

You take me where the water
Is quiet and cool and clear;
And there I rest and know I'm safe
For you are always near.

Lois Rock, based on Psalm 23

As our tropical sun gives forth its light, so let the rays from your face enter every nook of my being and drive away all darkness within.

Prayer from the Philippines

Lord, give us weak eyes for things which are of no account and clear eyes for all your truth.

Soren Kierkegaard (1813–55)

O thou great Chief, light a candle within my heart, that I may see what is therein and sweep the rubbish from thy dwelling-place.

An African schoolgirl's prayer

Lord God, you are my light in the darkness,
You are my warmth in the cold,
You are my happiness in sorrow.

Author unknown

May the sun shine warm on your face,
this day and evermore.

May the blessing of light be on you,
light without and light within.
May the blessed sunlight shine upon you
and warm your heart
till it glows like a great fire
and strangers may warm themselves
as well as friends.

And may the light
shine from your eyes,
like a candle
set in the windows of a home,
bidding the wanderer to come in
out of the storm.

Adapted from a traditional Irish blessing

A Close-of-Day Prayer of Reflection

At the end of the day take time to look back....
Ask God to help you see what God wants seen about the day.

Beginning with when you awoke,
play back the day, recalling events,
people, conversations.

Thank God for particular events of the day.
Notice: the good things...

And the difficult or upsetting things....
If there is anything you feel bad about and regret,
say sorry to God and ask for forgiveness.

Talk everything over with God; be honest
about the feelings of the day.

Now feel God's love wrapping
around you like a warm blanket.

Jesus, tender Shepherd, hear me,

Bless your little lamb tonight;

Through the darkness please be near me,

Keep me safe till morning light.

All this day your hand has led me,

And I thank you for your care;

You have warmed and clothed and fed me;

Listen to my evening prayer.

Mary L. Duncan (1814–40)

Sleep, my child, and peace attend thee,

All through the night;

Guardian angels God will send thee,

All through the night.

Soft the drowsy hours are creeping,

Hill and vale in slumber sleeping,

I my loving vigil keeping,

All through the night.

A traditional Welsh prayer

When I lie down, I go to sleep in peace;
you alone, O Lord, keep me perfectly safe.

Psalm 4:8

Dear Jesus, as a hen covers her chicks with her
wings to keep them safe, protect us this dark night
under your golden wings.

A prayer from India

Keep me as the apple of your eye;
hide me under the shadow of your wings.

Psalm 17:8

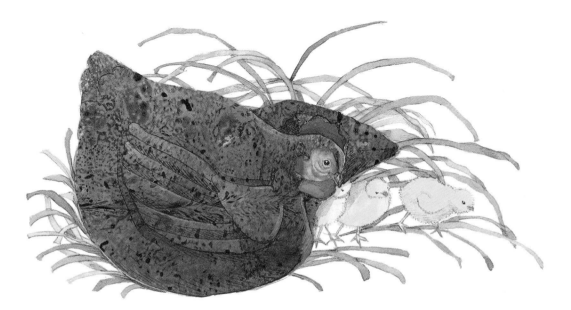

Go to sleep and good night;
In a rosy twilight,
With the moon overhead
Snuggle deep in your bed.
God will watch, never fear,
While Heaven draws near.

Karl Simrock (adapted by Louis Untermeyer)

Dear God,
Please protect me from nasty dreams
and scary thoughts.

For God is by me when I pray,
And when I close my eyes in sleep,
I know that he will with me stay,
And will all night watch by me keep.

Thomas Miller (1807-74)

For today, we thank you.
For tomorrow, we trust you.
For this night, we rest in you.
Amen

Dear God,
Thank you for being with me today.
Be with all my family near and far.
Watch over us this night, I pray.
Amen

God of the busy day;
God of the quiet night;
be with us now as we sleep.

Day is done,
gone the sun
from the lake,
from the hills,
from the sky.
Safely rest,
all is well!
God is nigh.

Author unknown

This is
the Day

There is a time for everything, and a
season for every activity under heaven.

Ecclesiastes 3:1

Through every minute of this day,

Be with me, Lord!

Through every day of this week,

Be with me, Lord!

Through every week of all this year,

Be with me, Lord!

Through all the years of this life,

Be with me, Lord!

So shall the days and weeks and years

Be threaded on a golden cord.

And all draw on with sweet accord

Unto thy fullness, Lord,

That so, when time is past,

By grace I may, at last,

Be with thee, Lord.

John Oxenham (1853–1941)

Lord, may I be wakeful at sunrise to begin a new day for you, cheerful at sunset for having done my work for you; thankful at moonrise and under starshine for the beauty of the universe. And may I add what little may be in me to your great world.

The Abbot of Greve

God of the past, present and future, our times are in your hands.
Watch over us we pray.
Amen

Dear God,

Thank you for our families and bless them, we pray.

Show us how to support and encourage one another.

Please be with us in all we do and share.

Lord God, please be with our families near and far,
protect them we pray.
Amen

I think about my father
(quietly offer your feelings to God).
Hear my prayer, Loving God.

I think about my mother
(quietly offer your feelings to God).
Hear my prayer, Loving God.

I think about the rest of my family
(quietly offer your feelings to God).
Hear my prayer, Loving God.

As I pray for my family so I pray for myself
that I might be a peacemaker.

May we love and understand each other, keep us from grumbling and complaining. Help us to see all the good things about our family life and not blame each other for the bad times. May we be quick to say thank you and slow to criticize.

Amen

God bless all those that I love;
God bless all those that love me;
God bless all those that love those that I love;
And all those that love those that love me.

From an old New England sampler

May the love of God our Father
Be in all our homes today:
May the love of the Lord Jesus
Keep our hearts and minds always:
May his loving Holy Spirit
Guide and bless the ones I love,
Father, mother, brothers, sisters,
Keep them safely in his love.

Author unknown

Dear God,
Fill our home with beautiful things:
Kind words
Warm welcomes
Fond goodbyes
Happy chatter
Easy silence
Togetherness
Space
Love.

Lois Rock

Unless the Lord builds the house,
those who build it labor in vain.

Psalm 127:1

Bless the four corners of this house,
And be the lintel blessed,
And bless the hearth and bless the board,
And bless each place of rest.

And bless the door which opens wide,
To strangers as to kin,
And bless each crystal window pane
That lets the sunshine in.

And bless the rooftree overhead,
And every sturdy wall—
The peace of man, the peace of God
The peace of love on all.

Author unknown

May the roof above never fall in,
may we below never fall out.

An Irish grace

For our food and those who prepare it:
For health and friends to share it,
We thank you, Lord.

Author unknown

Each time we eat,
may we remember God's love.

A prayer from China

For every cup and plateful,
God make us truly grateful.

A.S.T. Fisher

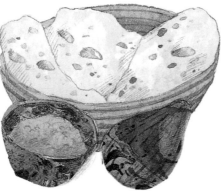

The bread is warm and fresh,
The water cool and clear.
Lord of all life, be with us,
Lord of all life, be near.

An African grace

Dear God,

We thank you for this food and for each other.

Amen

All good gifts around us

Are sent from heaven above,

Then thank the Lord, O thank the Lord,

For all his love.

Matthias Claudius (1740–1815), translated by
Jane Montgomery Campbell (1817–78)

We thank you, God, for this happy day,

for bright and sunny weather;

we thank you, God, for our food,

and time to be together.

For all the love and the laughter,
thank you, God.
For all we have explored and shared,
thank you, God.
For the times we've argued but made up,
thank you, God.
For this friendship,
we thank you, God.

Help us to remember that to have
a friend we need to be a friend.
Amen

Help me, O God, to be a good and true friend:
to be always loyal and never to let my friends down:
Never to talk about them behind their backs in a way
   which I would not do before their faces;
never to betray a confidence or talk about the things
   about which I ought to be silent;
always to be ready to share everything I have;
to be as true to my friends as I would wish them to be to me.
This I ask for the sake of him who is the greatest
   and truest of all friends, for Jesus' sake.

William Barclay (1907–78)

Loving God, help us to make friends
with people who bring out the best in
us and give us the courage to stand up
for what is right, good and fair.
Amen

Dear God, I sometimes feel
I have no friends. Please show me
what to do, and what to think
and say when I feel left out.

Lord God,

We pray for all who are sick. Especially we pray for... (mention anyone you wish to pray for). Please bring them peace in their time of suffering. Amen

Father, we commit to your loving care all children in hospitals. Comfort them as they miss the familiar surroundings of home. Take away their fear. Give gentleness and understanding to all who care for them. Hold them now in your safekeeping.

Mary Batchelor

For the skills of doctors and nurses,
thank you, God.
For medicines to make people better,
thank you, God.
For my family's loving care,
thank you, God.
For a comfy bed and a good book,
thank you, God.

Feeling poorly in my bed,
Feeling poorly in my head,
Feeling poorly, feeling pain:
God, please make me well again.

Lois Rock

Help me, kind God, to show your love and care
to my friends and family when they are ill.

Su Box

Help me not to pick over the past or worry about the future, but to live today, seeing the best in it and giving the most to it.
Amen

Dear God,
Please take today's unhappiness from me. I cannot change what happened, but help me to change how I feel about it. Show me what I can do to make things better.

God, give strength to those who are weak today and give hope to those in despair. Give light and love and peace and faith, and use us to show you are there.

O God, grant us the serenity
to accept what cannot be changed,
the courage to change what can be changed,
and the wisdom to know the difference.

Reinhold Niebuhr (1892–1971)

Lord, give us your peace this day and always.
Amen

My dearest Lord,

be thou a bright flame before me,

be thou a guiding star above me,

be thou a smooth path beneath me,

be thou a kindly shepherd behind me,

today and forevermore.

St. Columba (521–97)

On this day of celebration, our hearts are full of thankfulness and praise. May the memory of today be a ray of sunshine on cloudy days.

Amen

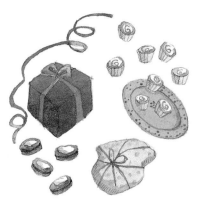

O God our Father, we would thank you for all the bright things of life. Help us to see them, and to count them, and to remember them, that our lives may flow in ceaseless praise; for the sake of Jesus Christ our Lord.

J.H. Jowett (1841–1923)

Dear God, you have given so much to me,
give one thing more—a grateful heart;
not thankful when it pleases me, as if your blessings had spare days;
but such a heart, whose very pulse may be your praise.

George Herbert (1593–1633) (adapted)

I give you thanks, O Lord, with my whole heart.

Psalm 138:1

Today is my birthday and I'm excited.
Help me to love those around me.
Help me to thank those who help me.
Help me to share and say thank you.

Sue Atkinson

For this great day of happiness, thank you, God.
For this exciting day of fun, thank you, God.
For this day of love and laughter, thank you, God.

Dear God,

Thank you for the wind.

For the wind that blows in the trees

And bends their branches to the ground.

The wind that blows the big sailing boats at sea,

And the little ones on the pond.

For the wind that blows the blossom, like snow, in the spring

And blows the leaves to the ground in the autumn.

Thank you for the wind that blows in my hair

And all around me.

Virginia Salmon

Dear God,

Thank you for the rain.

For the rain that runs and trickles down the window

And makes patterns on the glass.

For the rain that makes the crops and flowers grow

And gives us water to drink....

Thank you for the rain which makes big puddles

In which we can jump.

Dear God, thank you for the rain.

Virginia Salmon

Dear God,

Thank you for the sun.

For the sun that warms our world

and makes the flowers grow.

The great golden sun brings life and light.

Thank you for sunny days of fun and

laughter.

Thank you for the sun.

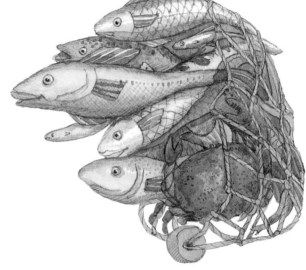

We plough the fields, and scatter
The good seed on the land,
But it is fed and watered
By God's almighty hand;
He sends the snow in winter,
The warmth to swell the grain,
The breezes and the sunshine,
And soft, refreshing rain:
All good gifts around us
Are sent from heaven above,
Then thank the Lord, O thank the Lord,
For all his love.

Matthias Claudius (1740–1815), translated by
Jane Montgomery Campbell (1817–78)

Sing to the Lord of harvest,
Sing songs of love and praise;
With joyful hearts and voices
Your alleluias raise.
By him the rolling seasons
In fruitful order move;
Sing to the Lord of harvest,
A joyous song of love.

J.S.B. Monsell (1811–75)

Dear God,
Give us grateful hearts for all that you give us.
Give us generous hearts, aware of the needs
of others.

Father in heaven, all good gifts come from you.
You send the sunshine and the rain, and
it is through your love and care that we can enjoy
harvest time. Thank you for providing
so richly for our needs and help us to share
the good things we have with those
who have little or nothing.
We pray for your blessing on every
kind of harvest that we enjoy. Thank
you for the harvest of the land and the
sea. Bless, too, the harvest of factory,
mine and workshop. Bless the harvest of
research and of creative art. May we work
together with you in every area of life to produce
what is worthwhile, good and fruitful. May you be
glorified in it all.

Mary Batchelor

Kindly Jesus,

You were born in a stable.

Be with those of us who live in shabby places.

You were born on a journey.

Be with those of us who are searching for a home.

You were given gold and richest gifts.

Be with those of us who have plenty.

You brought the light of heaven to earth.

Bring your light to all of us this Christmas.

Lois Rock

Jesus, heralded by the angels,

help us to see you more clearly.

Jesus, visited by the shepherds,

help us to follow you more nearly.

Jesus, adored by the wise men,

help us to love you more dearly.

This Christmas time and evermore.

Amen

Dear God,

Help us to remember that Christmas is all about you; that it is your birthday. As we enjoy all the wonderful treats of this season, may we know your love and share it with others.

Amen

We thank you, God, for Christmas:

For all the excitement and anticipation,
   we thank you, God.

For shining decorations and tall fir trees,
   we thank you, God.

For presents, cards and favorite foods,
   we thank you, God.

For time with our family and friends,
   we thank you, God.

For giving us Jesus on that first Christmas
   long ago,
   we thank you, God.

Dear God,
Thank you for new opportunities and new beginnings.
Help us to make the best of this new start and to go
forward with confidence and joy.

Here I am, Lord,
At the end and the beginning—
The end of one life, beginning of another;
Leaving behind the well-known,
Well-worn, comfortable things
And stepping out into the unknown,
Unseen, unfamiliar.

It's scary, Lord,
This next stage of the journey—
Where does this road lead? Where will it end?
Walk with me, Jesus, hold my hand,
Be my companion on the journey
And together we'll step boldy
Into the unknown.

Rowena Edlin-White

Lord of the years, a new chapter is opening and my excitement is tinged with fear. Help me to remember that in all my comings and goings and through all the ups and downs you are a constant thread woven through everything.

Amen

For the year that is past, we thank you, God.
For the year to come, we trust you, God.

There is a green hill far away,
Outside a city wall,
Where the dear Lord was crucified
Who died to save us all.

We may not know, we cannot tell,
What pains he had to bear;
But we believe it was for us
He hung and suffered there.

Mrs. C.F. Alexander (1818–95)

Dear God,
We shudder as we picture the
cruelty and suffering on that dark
Friday long ago. Thank you for
loving us. Thank you for Jesus.
Thank you that Good Friday is
not the end of the story.

Loving God, we come to you with all the
brokenness around us—broken dreams,
broken promises and broken hearts. Jesus,
broken on the cross, we come to you: you
alone can make us whole.

Come, Holy Angels,
into this dark night.
Roll away the stone of death.
Let the light of life
shine from heaven.

Lois Rock

Dear God,
May the sadness
of Good Friday
make Easter Sunday
even more joyful.

Friday sunset, black and red.
Weep, for Jesus Christ is dead.
Sunday sunrise, white and gold.
Christ is risen, as foretold.

Lois Rock

Ring out the bells!
Shout it from the rooftops!
He is risen. Christ Jesus is risen in glory.
Ring out the bells!
Shout it from the rooftops!

Easter eggs,
Easter chicks,
Easter holiday,
Easter fun.
Thank you, God,
for this happy time.

Dear God,
We thank and praise you for the joy of
Easter when you rose from death to life.
Help us to remember that the light
of your love is with us even when
everything appears dark.

Jesus Christ is risen today.
Alleluia!

Dear God,

Sometimes I find it so hard to do the right thing. Even when I know I shouldn't, I end up making the wrong choice. Often I am not brave enough to stand up for what I know to be right. Help me to be stronger and please show me the way to go.

Dear Father,

When we are tempted to be unkind,

When we are tempted to be unfair,

When to others' troubles we are blind,

Remind us how we would feel, and make us care.

Jack and Edna Young

Dear God,

We are sorry for the wrong things we have done.

We are sorry for the wrong things we have said.

For the wrong in our hearts, please forgive us

and help us to live as you want us to.

All that we ought to have thought and have not thought,

All that we ought to have said and have not said,

All that we ought to have done and have not done,

All that we ought not to have spoken and yet have spoken,

All that we ought not to have done, and yet have done,

For these words, and works, pray we, O God, for forgiveness.

Traditional

Dear God,

A new term is beginning. May it be for us a fresh start.

Help us to enter this term with enthusiasm and determination.

May we be happy in our work and play.

Thank you for our school—
for the fun we have;
for the work we do;
for the friends we share.
Help us to work together to
make our school a place of
happiness, love and respect.
Amen

O Lord, bless our school;
that, working together
and playing together,
we may learn more about you,
ourselves and one another.

Why are Monday mornings so difficult, God? It's hard to get up, hard to remember my books, hard to find my homework. Help me not to be too grumpy going back to school after the weekend.

Bullies:
They say, "We're only teasing."
But it's not a joke to me.

They say, "We're only playing."
But it's not a game to me.

They say, "We don't mean anything nasty."
But, O God, that's not true.
That's not true.

Lois Rock

Dear God,
Make me deaf to the things bullies say and give me the courage to tell someone. Show me who to ask for help.
Amen

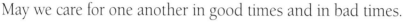

Help us to work as a team.

May we respect one another for our different talents.

Help us to work as a team.

May we enable one another to do the best we can.

Help us to work as a team.

May we care for one another in good times and in bad times.

Lois Rock

Thank you, God, for the fun of running, jumping, skipping. Thank you for bodies which can do such amazing things.

Dear God,

I'm not very good at sports. I always get picked last for team games. My body just doesn't seem to do what others find so easy. Help me to be brave and not worry, and also to remember that no one can be good at everything.

When I win, help me not to boast.
When I lose, help me not to sulk.

Tennis racket, baseball bat,
rugby football, riding hat,
swimming costume, cricket stumps,
cycling helmet, skateboard jumps.
O Lord, for these and all our fun
we thank you each and every one.

Christopher Herbert, prayer of a British school child

Dear God,
Be with those who travel
Protect them on their way
Bless them with good weather
Each and every day.

Dear God,
This vacation is not turning out the way I wanted it to. All the excitement I felt has now gone and I feel disappointed. Will you show me, God, how to find the good things here and how to make the most of this time? I don't want to spoil the vacation for others. Thank you, God.
Amen

As I sit on the beach and look out to sea, as I breathe in the fresh breezy air, as my toes burrow in the golden sand, as I feel the morning sunlight bathing me in warmth, I think of you, God, and my heart is full of thanks.

Thank you, God, for summer days and vacation fun,
for adventures and new experiences.

Time to be together,
time to laugh and talk;
for this time as a family
we thank you, loving God.

The stones are smoothed by constant storms at sea and they sit here now, reminding me that as I grow up and learn more about life, corners will get knocked off me.

The shells are homes of animals now gone, new ones now teeming in the sea. Life and death are all around me and sometimes I feel afraid. But you are there, God, holding on to me, leading me on through my life.

The seaweed fronds wave in the water, food you have provided for the rich life of the sea. Thank you that you provide all that I need, dear Lord.

The water at the moment is calm, rocking gently to and fro. But within the great mystery of your creation, that same water can be treacherous. Help me to lean on you through all the storms my life might bring.

The wind is gently touching me, telling me of your loving spirit. Help me to feel your spirit and to trust in you for all that lies ahead.

Sue Atkinson

All Our Tomorrows

Christ, let me see you in others,
Christ, let others see you in me.
Christ, let me see:
You are the caller,
You are the poor,
You are the stranger at my door.
You are the wanderer,
The unfed,
You are the homeless
With no bed.
You are the man driven insane,
You are the child
Crying in pain.
You are the one who comes to me.
Open my eyes that I may see.

David Adam

Isn't it strange how princes and kings,
and clowns that caper in sawdust rings,
and common people, like you and me,
are builders for eternity?

R.L. Sharpe (c.1870–c.1950)

Dear God,
In a world that could do with a lot more love
and a lot less hate, show me how to spread
your love and goodness.
Amen

Unbidden came God's love,
Not rushing from the skies
As angel, flame or dove,
But shining through your eyes.

Thomas H. Troeger

Dear God,

When everything is going wrong I sometimes wonder why you let
bad things happen. But then you open my eyes to the majesty of
your world, and I know once more that you are far greater than
I can imagine, and I believe once more that your love and goodness
will not be overcome.

Lois Rock, based on the book of Job

Why the collapsing buildings?
Why the dying people?
Why when they had so little?
Why should they have nothing?

Why did he go to help?
Why did she care for him?
Why did you give that money?
Why do I cry for a stranger?

Thank you, God, for all the people
who have the courage and skills to
help when disaster strikes. The world
is a better place because of them.

Jesus, as a mother you gather your people to you:

you are gentle with us as a mother with her children;

often you weep over our sins and our pride:

tenderly you draw us from hatred and judgment.

You comfort us in sorrow and bind up our wounds:

in sickness you nurse us,

and with pure milk you feed us.

St. Anslem (1033–1109)

God is our refuge and strength,

a very present help in trouble.

Psalm 46:1

God of all people,
This week on TV they have been showing pictures
of refugees. Some of the children were crying, God, and they looked
so hungry. I'm not very old, but will you show me a way to help them?
I know that your love is with them and I would like to show them love, too.
Amen

Betty Shannon Cloyd

Make your circle around the poor, God of love;
make your circle around the hungry, God of compassion;
make your circle around the oppressed, God of liberation;
make your circle around the victims of war, God of peace.

John Johansen-Berg

We pray for the children of the world who live in hunger, with disease or in danger and fear. We know it's not fair that some of us should have so much and others so very little. Help us to stand up for what is right and to be people of love and generosity. Loving God, show us your way.

Why do babies starve when there's enough food to feed the world? I may not be able to change the greed of others, but with your help, God, I can stop my own greed. Show me your ways of generosity and self-control.

May all the people of the world have everything they need.
Su Box

Lord, make me an instrument of your peace.
Where there is hatred, let me sow love;
Where there is injury, pardon;
Where there is discord, union;
Where there is doubt, faith;
Where there is despair, hope;
Where there is darkness, light;
Where there is sadness, joy;
For your mercy and your truth's sake.

Attributed to St. Francis of Assisi (1182–1226)

Lord God, we thank you for the
opportunities you give us to be
peacemakers. Help us, we pray,
to have the courage to act with
love and compassion.
Amen

Dear God,

Let there be peace on earth and let it begin with me. Help me to love my family and my friends as you would have me love. Let me love even those who are unlovable, those who are different from me. Help me to love them as I love myself.

Amen

Betty Shannon Cloyd

God our Father, Creator of the world,
please help us to love one another.
Make nations friendly with other nations;
make all of us love one another like brothers and sisters.
Help us to do our part to bring peace in the world
and happiness to all people.

A Prayer from Japan

Nation from nation, white from black,
rich from poor, old from young:
we offer you our divided world
and ask for your healing.

O God of many names
Lover of all nations
We pray for peace
in our hearts
in our homes
in our nations
in our world.
The peace of your will
The peace of our need.

George Appleton

As the earth keeps turning, hurtling through space, and night falls and day breaks from land to land, let us remember people—waking, sleeping, being born and dying—one world, one humanity. Let us go from here in peace.

World Council of Churches

Help us to love one another and make this world more like heaven.

Su Box

I had a paint box
but it didn't have the color red
for the blood of the wounded,
nor white
for the hearts and faces of the dead.

It didn't have yellow either
for the burning sands of the desert.

Instead it had orange
for the dawn and the sunset
and blue
for new skies
and pink
for the dreams of young people.

I sat down and painted peace.

A prayer by a ten-year-old from Latin America

May we learn to appreciate different points of view:

to know that the view from the hill is
    different from the view in the valley;
the view to the east is different from the
    view to the west;
the view in the morning is different from
    the view in the evening;
the view of a parent is different from the
    view of a child;
the view of a friend is different from the
    view of a stranger;
the view of humankind is different from
    the view of God.

May we all learn to see what is good, what is true,
what is worthwhile.

Lois Rock

Dear God,

Save us from thinking that we have all the answers.

Save us from talking when we should be listening.

Save us from clenched fists and closed minds.

Open our hearts to the way of peace.

Amen

Lord all power is yours

The power of the atom is yours

The power of the spacecraft is yours

The power of the computer is yours

The power of the jet is yours

The power of television is yours

The power of electricity is yours

Lord all power is yours

On loan it is ours

Lord let us use it aright

That it reveal your might

Lord all power is yours.

David Adam

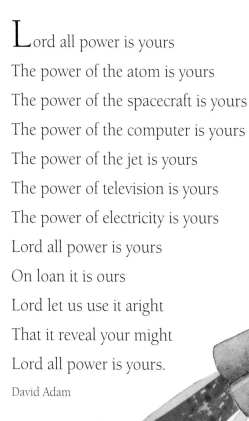

O God, help us not to despise or oppose what we do not understand.

William Penn (1644–1718)

Dear God,

Thank you for giving us creative, inquiring minds capable of amazing discoveries. We thank you for all those who use their intelligence to improve our lives.

Amen

I see the rubbish in the street,
smoke in the air,
and the fish gasping in polluted rivers.

I turn to you, Lord of all Creation,
asking you to forgive us.

Help us to care for your beautiful world,
to love, protect and nurture it,
so that the plants and animals will flourish,
and all creation will sing of your greatness.

Sue Atkinson

Plastic bag floating on the lake.
Plastic bag floating with the ducks.
Plastic bag; our calling card.
Forgive us, God of Creation.

We waste so much, God.
We waste food.
We waste money.
We waste time.
We waste the precious gifts you have given us.
Help us to want less, to consume
and squander less and to treat the world you
have given us with care and respect.

Lord God, help us to play our part
in caring for our world. Help us to
see where we can begin to make a
difference. Never let us think that it
is pointless to care.
Amen

In war, in tragedy, in dark, tough times
help us to remember your constant love
and to keep praying and working for the
world to be as you intended.

Hope is a candle we hold up
against the darkness.

Peace is not simply an absence of armed conflict.

Peace is not simply an absence of conflict.

Peace is not simply an absence of arms.

Peace is not simply an absence.

Peace is not simply.

Peace is not.

Peace is.

Peace.

Elizabeth Birtles

Everlasting Peace

The Lord will settle disputes between great nations....
They shall beat their swords into ploughs
and their spears into pruning-hooks;
nations will never again go to war,
never prepare for battle again.

Based on Isaiah 2:4

Everyone will live in peace among
their own vineyards and fig trees and
no one will make them afraid.

Based on Micah 4:4

Let us walk in the light which the
Lord gives us.

Isaiah 2:5

Jesus' Words of Peace and Reconciliation

O God, sometimes I feel as if nowhere is safe anymore.
I worry at night. I am fearful in the day. Where can I run to?
Where can I hide?

   Jesus says:

Come to me when the weight of
your worries and fears bears down on you;
tell me everything and I will lift
the load from you.

Based on Matthew 6:34

Peace I leave with you, my peace
I give to you; not as the world gives
do I give to you. Let not your heart
be troubled, neither let it be afraid.

John 14:27

My command to you is to love one another.

John 15:17

Love your enemies, do good to those who hate you, bless those who curse you, pray for those who treat you badly.

Luke 6:27–28

Blessed are the peacemakers,
for they will be called children of God.

Matthew 5:9

Treat others as you would like people to treat you.

Luke 6:31

The Prayer Jesus Taught Us

Our Father in heaven,
hallowed be your name,
your kingdom come,
your will be done,
on earth as in heaven.
Give us today our daily bread.
Forgive us our sins
as we forgive those who sin against us.
Lead us not into temptation
but deliver us from evil.
For the kingdom, the power
and the glory are yours
now and forever.
Amen

Like a loving parent you
watch over us.
We pray that your heavenly
goodness and love may
be seen everywhere.
May all the people of the
world have what they need
to be truly happy.
And when we fail to live according
to your loving ways, please
forgive us. Help us not to
give in to the desire to do things
we know to be wrong;
keep us from harm.
when we are wronged, may we learn to forgive.
You are in control now and forever.
Amen

God of all people, encircle our fragile world with your love, peace and justice.

Dear God,

May we, the children of the world, not repeat the mistakes of past generations. Free us from the traps of old arguments and ancient battles.

May we, the children of the world, discover a new way of living, where the riches of some are not at the expense of others.

May we, the children of the world, use our energy and optimism to overcome the barriers and fences of the past.

May we, the children of the world, have a new vision for this planet, so that we waste less and conserve more.

May we, the children of the world, live in harmony with you, your creation and each other.

Amen

May the Lord bless you and take care of you;
May the Lord be kind and gracious to you;
May the Lord look on you with favor and give
you peace.

Numbers 6:24–26

The grace of the Lord Jesus Christ,
and the love of God,
and the fellowship of the Holy Spirit
be with you all.

2 Corinthians 13:13

Bless to us, O God, the doors we open, the
thresholds we cross, the roads that lie before us.
Go with us as we go and welcome us home.

The Iona Community

God the Father, bless us;
God the Son, defend us;
God the Spirit, keep us
now and evermore.

Author unknown

May the Lord himself, who is our source of peace,
give you peace at all times and in every way.

2 Thessalonians 3:16

Blessing and laughter and loving be yours
The love of a great God who names you and holds you
While the earth turns and the flowers grow
This day
This night
This moment
And forever.

Angela Ashwin

Go, and know that the Lord goes with you:

let God lead you each day

into the quiet place of your heart,

where he will speak with you;

know that he loves you and watches over you—

that he listens to you in gentle understanding,

that he is with you always,

wherever you are and however you may feel:

and the blessings of God—Father, Son

and the Holy Spirit—be yours forever.

Amen

Index of First Lines and Phrases

E

F

Subject Index

Acknowledgments

Thanks go to all those who have given permission to include material in this book, as indicated in the list below. Every effort has been made to trace and contact copyright owners. We apologize for any inadvertent omissions or errors.

All uncredited prayers are copyright © Rebecca Winter.
David Adam: pp. 15, 136 from *The Edge of Glory*. p. 64 from *The Rhythm of Life*. p. 124 from *The Cry of the Deer*. Used by permission of SPCK and Morehouse Publishing. **Dave Andrews:** p. 34, Copyright © Dave Andrews. **Angela Ashwin:** p. 149 taken from *Book of 1000 Prayers* – Zondervan Edition Copyright © 1996, 2002 by Angela Ashwin. Used by permission of The Zondervan Corporation. **Sue Atkinson:** pp. 17, 36, 46, 53, 61, 62, 100, 122. Copyright © Sue Atkinson. **George Appleton:** p. 132 from *The Oxford Book of Prayer* © 1985 Oxford University Press. Reproduced by permission. **William Barclay:** p. 95 Copyright © the estate of William Barclay. **Mary Batchelor:** pp. 22, 96, 105. Copyright © Mary Batchelor. **John L Bell:** p. 19 "Send out your light, Lord," p. 20 "Listen Lord, Listen Lord" Copyright © 1995, WGRG, Iona Community, Glasgow, G2 3DH, Scotland. **Elizabeth Birtles:** p. 140 from *Crying Out, Lord: an anthology of poetry and prose on women's spiritual insight and experience* (Unitarian Worship Subcommittee, London) **Su Box:** pp. 43, 97, 129, 133. Copyright © Lion Hudson plc. **Evelyn Francis Capel:** p. 45 from *Prayers and Verses for contemplation*. Reprinted by permission of Floris Books, Edinburgh. **Amy Carmichael:** pp. 14, 25, taken from *Mountain Breezes, the collected poems of Amy Carmichael*. Copyright © The Donhavur Fellowship. Published by CLC Publications, Fort Washington, PA, USA. Used by permission. **Lilian Cox:** p. 65 Reproduced from *What next, Lord?* with the permission of Christian Education. **H.W. Dobson:** p. 56 from *In excelsis*. Used by permission of the National Society for Promoting Religious Education. **John Drinkwater:** p. 52 from *The Collected Poems of John Drinkwater Vol 1, 1908–1917*. Published by permission of Samuel French Ltd on behalf of the Estate of John Drinkwater. **Rowena Edlin-White:** pp. 30, 108. Copyright © Rowena Edlin-White. **Eleanor Farjeon:** p. 32 "Morning has broken" taken from *The Children's Bells* published by Oxford University Press. Reproduced by permission of David Higham Associates Ltd. **AST Fisher:** p. 92 from *A Patchwork of Blessings and Graces* compiled by Mary Daniels. Copyright © 1996 Gracewing Publishers. **Christopher Herbert:** p. 119 taken from *The Prayer Garden* by Bishop Christopher Herbert. Copyright © 1995. Used by permission of the Zondervan Corporation. **John Johansen-Berg:** p. 128 taken from *Textures of Tomorrow* ed. Kate Compson. Copyright © John Johanses-Berg. **Elizabeth Laird:** p. 58 from *Prayers for Children* compiled by Christopher Herbert. Reprinted by permission of HarperCollins Publishers Ltd. **Madeleine L'Engle:** p. 33. Copyright © 1974 Madeleine L'Engle. Reprinted by permission of Lescher & Lescher Ltd. All rights reserved. **Kate McIlhagga:** p. 148 "Bless to us, O God" from *The Green Heart of the Snowdrop*. Copyright © 2004 Kate McIlhagga, Wild Goose Publications, Glasgow G2 3DH, Scotland www.ionabooks.com. **John Oxenham:** p. 86 taken from *Bees in Amber*. Copyright © John Oxenham. **Lois Rock:** pp. 16, 37, 75, 90, 97, 106, 111, 112, 118, 126, 135. Copyright © Lion Hudson plc. **Betty Shannon Cloyd:** pp. 128, 131. Copyright © Betty Shannon Cloyd. **Kenneth Steven:** p. 59. Copyright © Kenneth Steven. **Thomas Troeger:** p. 125 Words by Thomas Troeger © 1994 Oxford University Press, Inc. Reproduced by permission. **Steve Turner:** p. 24. Copyright © Steve Turner. **Jack & Edna Young:** p. 115 Reproduced from *Praying with Juniors* with the permission of Christian Education.

Miscellaneous
p. 133 "As the earth keeps turning" from *Banquet of Praise*. Used by permission of The World Council of Churches.
p. 134 "I had a paintbox" from *Lifelines, Words and Pictures for Prayer and Reflection* published by Christian Aid.
p. 148 "God the Father bless us" from *Little Folded Hands* by Allan H Jahsmann. Copyright © 1959, 1987 Concordia Publishing House. All Rights Reserved. Used by permission.

pp. 22, 29, 90, 127: Scripture quotations are from the New Revised Standard Version published by HarperCollins Publishers, copyright © 1989 by the Division of Christian Education of the National Council of the Churches of Christ in the USA, and are used by permission. All rights reserved.

pp. 34, 74, 81, 141, 148, 149: Scripture quotations are from the Good News Bible published by The Bible Societies/HarperCollins Publishers, copyright © 1966, 1971, 1976, 1992 American Bible Society.

pp. 72, 81, 86, 100: Scripture quotations taken from the Holy Bible, New International Version, copyright © 1973, 1978, 1984 International Bible Society. Used by permission of Zondervan and Hodder & Stoughton Limited. All rights reserved. The "NIV" and "New International Version" trademarks are registered in the United States Patent and Trademark Office by International Bible Society. Use of either trademark requires the permission of International Bible Society. UK trademark number 1448790.

pp. 142: The New King James Version copyright © 1982, 1979 Thomas Nelson, Inc.